世界自然遗产

WORLD NATURAL HERITAGE

黄　龙

HUANG LONG

松潘县旅游局·黄龙风景区管理局·中国旅游出版社 编

中国旅游出版社

人间瑶池　(摄影:谭明)
Jasper Lake under Heaven

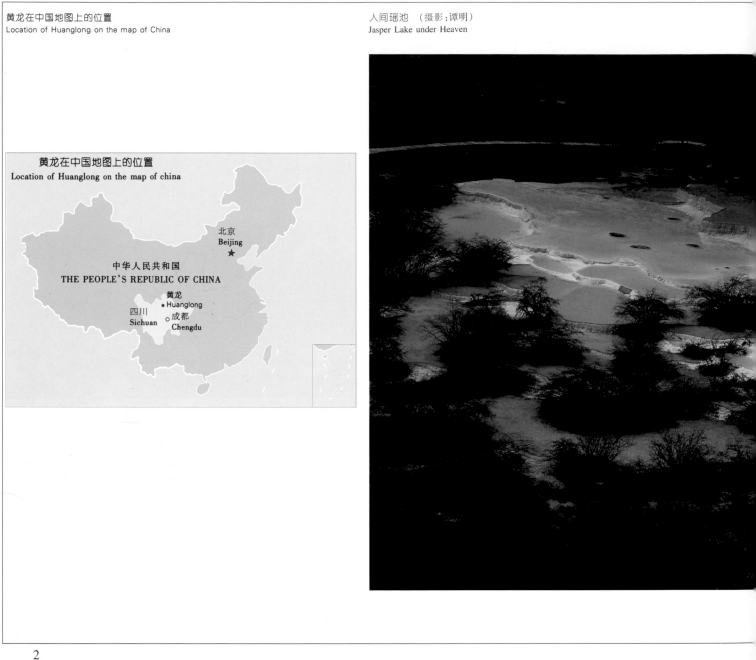

黄龙在中国地图上的位置
Location of Huanglong on the map of china

北京
Beijing
★

中华人民共和国
THE PEOPLE'S REPUBLIC OF CHINA

黄龙
● Huanglong

四川
Sichuan

○ 成都
Chengdu

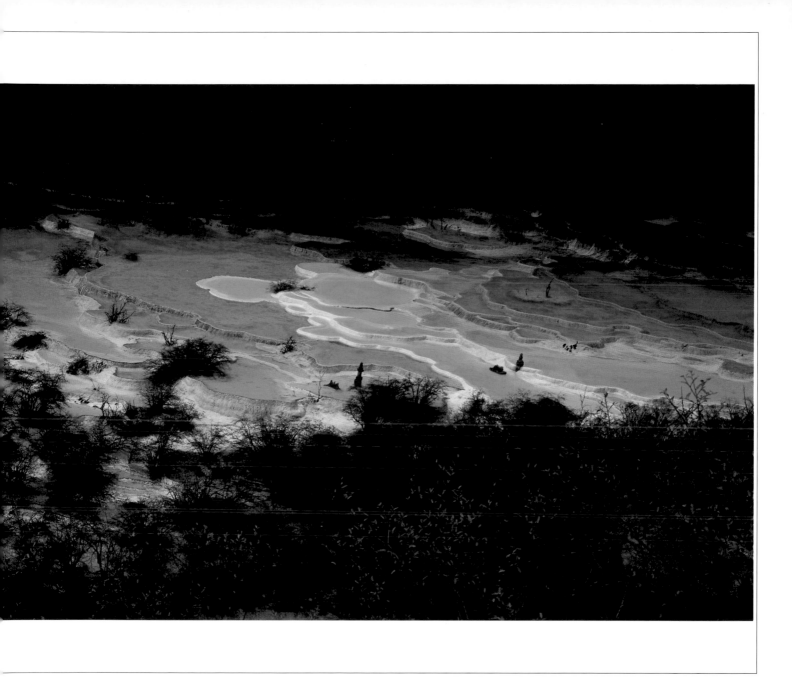

话说黄龙
Hanglong: On the Verge of a Takeoff

即使是到过黄龙的人也常常将景区的名字搞错,一些新闻媒体也是如此,不是说成"黄龙寺",就是叫做"黄龙洞"。或许是因为在中国传统文化中,黄龙是神而非地名,倘若是地名,就非得和道观、庙宇、洞穴等连在一起,如浙江杭州和湖南张家界的黄龙洞,一个是道教的福地,一个是天然溶洞;或许是因为这个景区内既有黄龙寺,而且还是上中下三个,又有黄龙洞,并且是中国最大的钙华洞穴;或许是因为它刚刚开放时就与九寨沟出双入对,人们总是将两者连在一起,三个字容易对应。但实实在在的,这个景区的名字只有两个字——黄龙。

有关黄龙的得名有两种说法:一是景以寺名,寺以神名。传说远古助禹治水的黄龙功成身退,隐居于此,修炼成仙而去;一是黄龙主景是一条从山顶逶迤而下的露天黄色钙华堆积体,上面彩池层层叠叠,登高远望,酷似一条五彩斑斓的金色巨龙自皑皑雪峰、莽莽丛林腾空而起,故名。两种说法都与传说中象征中华民族的"龙"密切相关。

黄龙地处青藏高原最东端,位于四川省阿坝藏族羌族自治州松潘县境内,南距省会成都 300 公里,与另一著名景区九寨沟接壤,分属两个不同的县,靠近四川、甘肃、陕西三省交界之地。景区面积 700 平方公里(另有外围保护区 640 平方公里),海拔 1800 米至 5588 米,其中主景区黄龙沟海拔 3100 米至 3500 米。气候和植被呈明显的垂直分布,属典型的高原温带——亚寒带季风气候。冬季漫长,春秋相连,基本上没有夏天,年平均气温 5－12 摄氏度,年温差和日温差都很大,人们常用"早穿棉衣午穿纱,抱着火炉吃西瓜"来形容这里的气候特征。

就像龙的形象是由蛇身、鱼鳞、鹿角等组合而成一样,黄龙景区是由黄龙沟、牟尼沟、雪宝鼎、丹云峡和松潘古城构成的。

这是一个神奇的地方,虔诚的藏族同胞把它奉为神山圣地,叫做"东日瑟尔嵯",意思是"东方的海螺沟和金色的海子";每年农历六月十五日至二十五日都要在这里举办盛大的庙会,转山朝拜。

高高的雪山,沐浴着太阳的光辉,溶出清清溪流,岷江从这里发源,向南越过广袤的成都平原,哺育出一个"天府之国"。滚滚的江流倾倒无数中国古人,使他们误认为它是长江的正源;涪江从此地起步,滔滔不绝,奔向太阳升起的地方……

一千多年前,为了藏汉民族的和睦,大唐王朝的文成公主远嫁拉萨从这里走过,在川主寺旁的一块石头上驻足回首,留下深深的足印……

二十世纪三十年代,中国工农红军"爬雪山,过草地"来过这里,这支军队的指挥者、一位名叫毛泽东的伟人登高远望,豪情满怀,孕育了"更喜岷山千里雪,三军过后尽开颜"的豪迈诗句,为白莽莽的雪山披上革命而浪漫的色彩……

当然,黄龙景区的出名,主要还是得益于它独特的地表钙华岩溶风光:

在终年积雪的雪宝鼎下,有一条古冰川塑造、相对高差 400 余米的沟槽,不知从什么时候开始,大量被雪水溶解了的地下碳酸钙渗出地表,长期沉积,形成了一条长达 3.6 公里、宽 30－170 米的巨型钙华堆积体。钙华体上,分布着大大小小 3400 多个钙华彩池和长达 2.5 公里的巨大钙华滩流以及众多的钙华瀑布、钙华洞穴。清冽的雪水沿钙华体漫流,层层跌落,穿林、过池、越堤、滚滩,注入涪江源流。层层彩池,莹红澜绿,如鱼鳞叠布,似梯田层列,呈八组分布,形态各异。有的流水丁冬,似迎宾曲悠扬悦耳;有的争奇斗艳,像五彩云霞异彩纷呈。条条钙滩,晶莹透明,飞珠溅玉;道道梯瀑,泻翠流垂,巧妙地构成一条活灵活现的金色巨龙,腾游于茫茫原始森林、皑皑雪峰和蓝天白云之间。这景色与传说中中国女神之王西王母的住所极其相似,被誉为"人间瑶池"。

世界上,石灰岩溶洞很多,地下钙华景观很容易看到,而像黄龙这样享受阳光雨露的地表钙华,由于成因相当复杂,极其稀少。迄今为止,被发现的类似景观还有美国黄石公园的钙华彩池群和与黄龙相像的黑水卡龙沟;不过,黄石公园的钙华规模不大,而卡龙沟的发育尚不完整。像黄龙这样发育完整、类型齐全、规模巨大的钙华景观,不仅在中国诸多风景名胜区中独树一帜,即便是在世界上,也是罕见的。1992 年,两位金发碧眼的风景专家,一位叫杰姆·塞尔,一位叫 P·H·C 卢卡斯,受联合国教科文组织的委托来此考察,被眼前绝妙的风光深深折服,赞叹"这里堪称世界上无与伦比的钙华奇观"。

除此之外,黄龙的雪峰、峡谷、森林和民族风情也极富魅力,一些人将它们与彩池一道并称为黄龙"五绝"。

雪宝鼎是岷山山脉的主峰,海拔 5588 米,被亘古不化的冰雪包裹着,像一座银色的金字塔,在群峰中巍然耸立,直刺苍穹。周围冰川垂悬,群峰林立,是中国最东部的现代冰川保存区。冰川下广泛发育着高山草甸,冰峰绿原,相互映衬。雪宝鼎山势险峻,1986 年 8 月 6 日才被中日联合登山队第一次征服,之后尚无人再攀。络绎不绝的朝山者只在山麓或山中仰望"神山"……

黄龙沟口,沿涪江源流而下,自玉笋峰至

扇子洞,两山夹峙,壁立千仞,怪石嵯峨,泉瀑飞泻,林荫蔽日,绵延15公里,垂直高差1378米,熔张家界的峰丛和长江三峡的峡谷风光于一炉,石马关、凌水岩、铅字牌……,接踵而至,构成一幅长长的自然山水画廊。每到秋天,满山红叶此淡彼浓,好似丹云满峡,扶壁穿林,故名丹云峡……

距黄龙沟15公里的牟尼沟,主要由扎尕瀑布和二道海组成。扎尕瀑布有"中国最大的钙华瀑布"之称,在巨大的钙华基座上,一道宽35米的水流分级倾泻而下,每跌落一级,就迸射出一簇簇晶莹的水花;中有水帘洞,下有堰塞湖,落差达93.7米,声震数里。二道海有天鹅海、百花海、犀牛群海等高山湖泊和煮珠温泉、翡翠矿泉。牟尼沟地区林海茫茫,不论是壮观的扎尕瀑布,还是静碧的湖泊、神奇的温泉,全都掩映在参天的密林之中。密林中原始物种繁多,常有大熊猫、金丝猴、牛羚等珍稀动物出没……

松潘是一座具有2000多年历史的古城,唐宋边塞的硝烟已经散尽,但明代厚厚的城墙和高高的城楼却依然保存完好。自古以来,藏、羌、回、汉各民族就在此共同居住,繁衍生息。炽热的阳光,铸就了当地人铜墙铁壁般的肤色和刚烈火热的性格;广漠的原野,孕育了他们对自然的崇拜和对宗教的虔诚。永无穷尽的转经、永远飘飞的经幡、永不停歇的礼拜和神秘的喇嘛庙、古朴的清真寺相得益彰,构成了一道亮丽的风景线……

如此迷人的风光,备受人们的推崇。美国西部国家公园管理局局长斯坦尼·欧伯特来到这里,写下这样的评语:"这里有似加拿大的雪山、怀俄明州的原始森林、科罗拉多的峡谷、黄石公园的钙华彩池,多类景观,集中一地,世所罕见。黄龙不仅是中国人民的宝

贵财富,也是全人类的。"过去,黄龙一直隐藏在深山里面,默默无闻,真正向外界敞开胸怀,还是最近二十年的事情:1982年,黄龙成为国家首批重点风景名胜区;1990年在全国四十佳风景名胜区评比中,与九寨沟一道并列新自然景区榜首;1992年,与九寨沟、武陵源(张家界)一起被纳入《世界自然遗产名录》,成为我国首批世界自然遗产单位。而今这里宾馆饭店拔地而起,通讯交通四通八达,中外游人纷至沓来。1998年,九寨沟、黄龙旅游环线公路改造竣工,一条宽敞平坦的大道从成都修到了黄龙;同时,一座现代化的旅游机场在川主寺旁破土动工,波音飞机将伴随着新世纪的脚步在这里降落。正如人们所期待的那样,沉寂千百万年的黄龙正在腾飞。

The press, and even those who have been to Huanglong (meaning: Yellow Dragon), often mistake the name "Huanglong" (meaning: "Yellow Dragon") for the name of a temple or cave temple for the probable reason that in traditional Chinese culture, the Yellow Dragon is often associated with celestial beings – seldom is it used as the name of a place. Huanglongdong (Yellow Dragon Cave) in Hangzhou, Zhejiang Province, for example, is a sanctuary of the Huanglong (Yellow Emperor and Lao Zi) Sect of Taoism, and the Yellow Dragon Cave in Zhangjiajie, Hunan Province, is a natural limestone cave. The "Huanglong" in question is often mistaken for "Huanglongdong", perhaps because the place is home to three Yellow Dragon temples and a Yellow Dragon Cave that happens to be China's largest travertine cave. Or perhaps because it was opened to tourists at about the same time as the three – syllable Jiuzhaigou, people tend to call it Huang – long – dong. But in actual fact the name of the place consists of only two syllables: Huanglong.

There are two theories about the origin of the name of Huanglong. One is that the place is named after the Huanglong Temple. Legend has it that in remote antiquity, the Yellow Dragon settled here as a recluse after helping King Yu harnessing the rivers, and eventually achieved immortality. Another theory attributes the name to the main scenic sight of the place, a huge deposit of yellow travertine that is formed by the evaporation of water from the summit of a mountain and that meanders its way down the slope like a colourful golden dragon gyrating its way across snowy mountains and through dense forests. Both theories are relevant to the dragon that is a symbol of the Chinese nation.

Huanglong, which is under the jurisdiction of Songpan County in Sichuan Province's Ngawa Qiang Autonomous Prefecture, is situated on the easternmost tip of the Qinghai – Tibet Plateau. Chengdu, capital of Sichuan Province, is 300 kilometres to the south. The Jiuzhaigou Scenic Zone, belonging to another county, sits next to Huanglong, which is also in close proximity to where Sichuan, Gansu and Shanxi cross their boundaries. The Huanglong Scenic Resort covers 700 square kilometres (not including a 640 – square – kilometre peripheral nature reserve) at an elevation of 1,800 to 5,588 metres, and Huanglong Gully, the centrepiece of the scenic resort, is 3,100 – 3,500 kilometres above sea level. The climate and the vegetation are distributed vertically, and the entire place is typical of the highland Temperate Zone, where winter is long, spring and autumn are linked, and summer is unheard of, and where sunshine is plentiful. The average annual temperature is 5 – 12 degrees Celsius; the striking difference in annual and daily temperatures has prompted the saying that the local people is in the habit of "putting on cotton – padded clothes in the morning and wearing short – sleeves during the noontime, and sitting by a stove to eat water – melons."

Just like a dragon composed of a snake's body, a fish's scales and a deer's antlers, the Huanglong Scenic Resort comprises the Huanglong (Yellow Dragon) Gully, the Xuebaoding (Snowy Precious Caldron), Danyun (Crimson Cloud) Gorge, and the ancient city of Songpan.

Huanglong is a fascinating place. The Tibetans regard it as a holy land, and make it a point to hold a grand summons ceremony during the 15th through the 25th of the sixth lunar month and cumambulate the mountains in tribute to the Buddha.

Sparkling water runs gurgling down high snow mountains to form the headwaters of the Minjiang, a river that flows through the vast and fertile Chengdu Plain and nurtures the "Land of Abundance" – Sichuan. The tumbling Minjiang River has fascinated so many ancient Chinese men of consequences that they mistook it for the orthodox source of the Yangtze River. Huanglong is also where the Peijiang River rises and begins flowing east.

On her way to Lhasa more than a thousand years ago, Princess Wencheng of the Tang dynasty had stopped over at Huanglong, and left a pair of deep footprints in a stone as she looked over her shoulder and cast a longing glance in the direction of her homeland.

In 1935, the Red Army on the world – famous Long March passed by Huanglong. Mao Zedong was so impressed by Huanglong's mountains that he composed the line: "Mingshan's thousand li of snow joyously crossed/The three Armies march on, each face glowing." The Long March ushered the Chinese history into a new period of historical development.

The fame of Huanglong stems to a large extent from its unique travertine and limestone landform.

At the foot of the snow – clad Xuebaoding Mountain lies a gully 400 or so metres deep that was brought into being by ancient glaciers. In times immemorial, large quantities of calcium carbonate was dissolved by meltwater and seeped through earth's surface to form a huge travertine deposit 3.6 kilometres long and 30 – 170 metres wide. The deposit is studded with 3,400 or so pools and many caves, and streaked by many waterfalls and a 2.5 – kilometre – long stream. Meltwater flowing all over the travertine deposit tumbles down one cliff head after another, threads through forests, feeds ponds, overflows dykes, rolls across shallow places until it empties into the Peijiang River. The ponds, lying one atop the other, assume a hundred and one different colours and form what looks like a terraced field. The waterfalls emit a pleasant sound as they cascade like coloured clouds. The calcium – containing shoals are crystal clear to the extent of being transparent. The streams flow this way and that along courses that look like numerous golden dragons swimming in dense woods and between snowy peaks and a blue sky that is filled with blue clouds. The entire scenery is evocative of the dwelling place of the Queen Mother of the Western Paradise. Hence the nickname of the place: Jasper Lake of the Mundane World.

Limestone caves are a dome a dozen in this world, and so are underground travertine scenery. Surface travertine formations like that of Huanglong is a rarity for complex causes. Similar scenery is also found in the Yellowstone National Park of the United States, and the Heishuika Dragon Gully next to Huanglong. However, the travertine formation of the Yellowstone is small in scale, and that of Heishuika is underdeveloped. Huanglong's travertine scenery is unmatched in that it is well developed, comes in a complete array of types, and is monumental in size. In 1992, two UNESCO experts made an inspection tour of the place and, captivated by what they had seen, lauded Huanglong as an unparalleled travertine wonder in this world.

Huanglong's snowy peaks, deep ravines, green woods and exotic folklore are as fascinating as its travertine pools. Together they are known as the "five wonders" of Huanglong. Xuebaoding, the 5,588 – metre – high main peak of the Mingshan Mountain Range, is eternally enveloped in snow as it soars into the sky like a silver pyramid. Surrounded by glaciers and perpendicular peaks, the peak is a modern glacier reserve in the easternmost part of China. The glaciers, and the grasslands below them, set each other off in a most picturesque manner. The Xuebaoding Mountain is so precipitous that it was not until August 6, 1986 that it was first conquered by a Sino – Japanese Mountaineering Team. For pilgrims who arrive in a constant stream, however, the mountain is simply an untouchable, awesome spectacle. Water flows along the Huanglong Gully down the Peijiang River, and the 15 – kilometre stretch from the Jade Bamboo Shoot Peak to the Fan Cave is hemmed in between sheer peaks and grotesque – looking crags and its waterdrop is an impressive 1,378 metres. The mountain scenery of Zhangjiajie and the magnificence of the Three Gorges of the Yangtze River are merged here almost imperceptibly. A series of scenic spots, such as Stone Horse Pass, Rock of Overhanging Water, and "Type – Face Tablet", turn this place into a long scroll of landscape painting. In autumn, the place is dyed crimson by red leaves, and that is why it is also known as Crimson Cloud Gully. The Mouni Gully, fifteen kilometres from the Huanglong Gully, is where the Zhaga Waterfall and Erdaohai are situated. The Zhaga Waterfall, known as China's largest travertine waterfall, is a body of water 35 to 40 metres in width. As it leaps and tumbles down a tremendous travertine base, it thunders with unceasing din, breaks into several sections during an impressive drop of 93.7 metres, and sends up geysers of water droplets that sparkle under the sun. Hidden behind the middle of the waterfall is the Water Curtain Cave, and at the bottom of it lies the Yansai Lake. Erdaohai

15

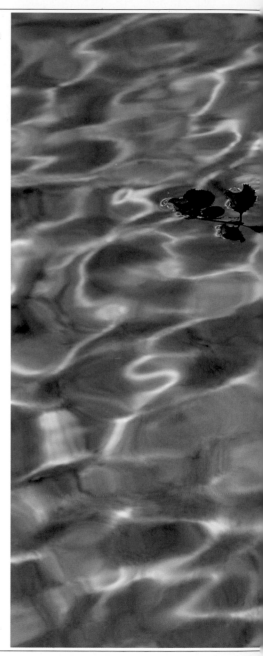

碧水秋波 （摄影:何世尧）
Autumn Scene: Ripples in a Limpid Pond

consists of such alpine lakes as Swan Lake, Hundred – Flower Sea and Rhinoceros Seas, as well as the Zhuzhu and Feicui springs. Muni Gully is cocooned under dense woods, and lakes and springs are tucked away in the shadows of towering trees. The woods are home to a good variety of wildlife, and teeming with giant pandas, snob – nosed golden monkeys and gnus.

Songpan is a historical city with a history of more than two thousand years. The smoke of war of the Tang and Song dynasties has long evaporated into thin air, but Songpan's Tang – dynasty city wall and gate towers are still in perfect condition. Tibetans, Qiangs, Huis and Hans have been living congenially in this place since ancient times. The resplendent sun has tempered the local people's brownish skin colour and fiery and forthright personality. The boundless wilderness has fostered their adoration for nature and their religious beliefs. Long queues of pilgrims spinning prayer wheels in their hands, fluttering sutra streamers, unending summons ceremonies, and mysterious Lamaist temples and ancient Islamic mosques, combine to render a fascinating aura to the local culture.

The charming landscape of Huanglong has not been lost on so many visitors. The director of the Western National Park Administration of the United States has this to say: In this place there are snow mountains such as can be seen in Canada, the primitive forests of Wyoming, the canyons of Colorado, the colourful travertine lakes of the Yellowstone National Park. Very few places in this world are in the possession of so many kinds of natural scenery. Huanglong is a precious asset not only of the Chinese people but also of the entire mankind. In the past, however, little was known about Huanglong. It was not until two decades ago that the place was opened to the outside world. In 1982, Huanglong was designated as one of China's first group of key scenic resorts. In 1990, Huanglong and Jiuzhaigou topped China's list of forty best scenic zones. In 1992, Huanglong was one of a group of Chinese scenic zones to appear on the UNESCO list of world natural heritages together with Jiuzhaigou and Wulingyuan. Many hotels and restaurants have been established in Huanglong to accommodate a constant stream of tourists from at home and abroad. In 1998, a wide and smooth highway was paved from Chengdu to Huanglong to facilitate a travel programme that includes Huanglong and Jiuzhaigou. Construction of a modern tourist airport has also come underway at the tableland of the Chuanzhu Temple, so that in the beginning of the next century Boeing aircraft will be able to gain access to Huanglong. After so many years of oblivion and seclusion, Huanglong today is poised for a takeoff like a real dragon.

黄龙奇观 （摄影:李天社）
A spectacular Scene at Huanglong

玉盘池 （摄影:何世尧）
Jade-Plate Pool

玉翠雪峰 （摄影:何世尧）
Snow-Clad Peaks

争艳池　（摄影:邱永东）
Rivaling-Colours Pool

莲台池 （摄影:高屯子）
Lotus Throne Pond

迎宾彩池　（摄影：胡斌）
Guest-Greeting Multiple-Hued Pond

金沙铺地 （摄影：高屯子）
Golden Sands

飞瀑流辉 （摄影：于宁）
A Cascading Waterfall

嬉　水　（摄影：胡斌）
Frolicing with Water

瑞雪映清波　（摄影：龚威健）
Rippling Water on a Snowy Land

碧水银滩 （摄影：林义平）
Limpid Water and Silvery Beach

洗身洞 （摄影：高屯子）
Body-Washing Cave

钙华波韵　（摄影:高屯子）
Charms of Calcareus

天光洒金滩 （摄影：龚威健）
Sunlight on the Golden Beach

水中盆景 （摄影:高晔）
Miniature Landscape in Water

盆景池 （摄影:陈锦）
A Pond of Miniature Landscapes

第 34 – 35 页图：含羞池 （摄影：何世尧）
Pp34 – 35：Shyness Pond

远眺争艳彩池 （摄影：高屯子）
The Rivaling-Colours Pool at a Distance

荷叶池 （摄影:何世尧）
Lotus-Leaf Pond

瑶池仙境 （摄影：高屯子）
A Wonderland Scene

右图：争艳彩池 （摄影：何世尧）
Right：Rivaling-Colours Pond

争艳池 （摄影：胡维标）
Colourful Pond

洗花池 （摄影：邱永东）
Flower-Washing Pond

洗花池　（摄影:龚威健）
Flower-Washing Pond

池水多变的色彩 （摄影:周孟琪 何世尧）
Colour-Conjuring Water in a Pond

池水多变的色彩 （摄影：何世尧）
Colour-Conjuring Water in a Pond

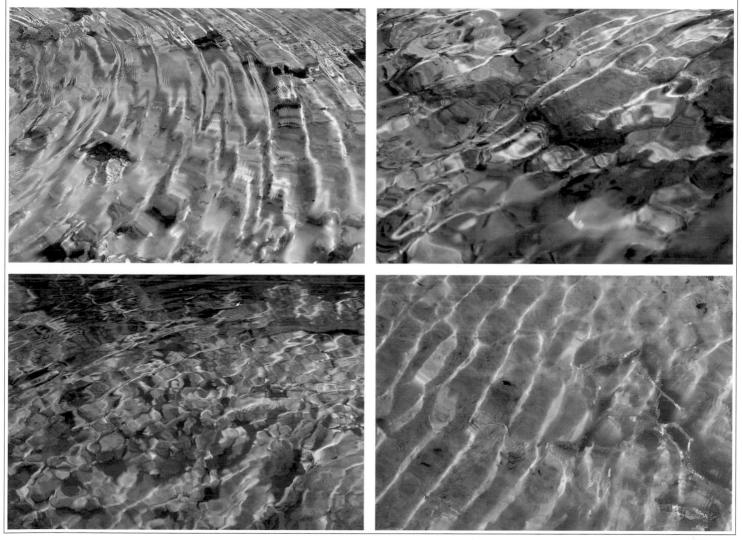

47

玉海蟾宫 （摄影:何世尧）
"Toad Palace in the Moon" in a Jade Sea

第 48 – 49 页图：映月彩池 （摄影:于宁）
Pp48 – 49: The Moon Mirrored in a Multiple-Hued
Pond

五彩池 （摄影：何世尧）
Five-Hued Pond

第 52 - 53 页图：五彩池 （摄影：于宁）
Pp52 - 53：Five-Hued Pond

初 雪 （摄影：高屯子）
After the First Snow Falls

石塔镇海 （摄影：高屯子）
Stone Pagoda Subduing the Sea

第 56 – 57 页图：雪山下的五彩池 （摄影：何世尧）
Pp56 – 57: A Multiple-Hued Pond below a Snow-clad
Mountain

第 58 页图：秋　水　（摄影：李杰）
P58: A Stream in Autumn
左上图：水中树　（摄影：林义平）
Top left: Trees Growing in a Pond
左下图：冰凌寒光　（摄影：米文岐）
Bottom left: Glistening Icicles

右上图：冰水交融　（摄影：胡斌）
Top right: Harmony Between Ice and Water
右下图：水下钙华　（摄影：邰永东）
Bottom right: Calcareus under Water

左上图：黄龙寺庙门 （摄影：李天社）
Top left：Front Gate of Huanglong Temple
左下图：石刻 （摄影：胡斌）
Bottom left：Stone Inscriptions
右图：石刻佛像 （摄影：泽仁珠）
Right：Stone Statue of the Buddha

左图：秋　叶 （摄影：高屯子）
Left：Fall leaves
右图：初　雪 （摄影：高屯子）
Right：After the First Snow Falls

晚　秋 （摄影：林义平）
A Late Autumn Scene

丹云峡 （摄影：杨继宗）
Danyun Gorge

左图：山林秋艳 （摄影：陈轲）
Left：The Colour of Autumn in a Mountain Forest
右图：峡谷激流 （摄影：高屯子）
Right：Rapids in a Ravine

环形瀑布 （摄影:高屯子）
A Circular Waterfall

第72-73页图：牟尼沟二道海 （摄影：何世尧）
Pp72-73：Erdaohai, Muni Gully

天鹅湖 （摄影：邰永东）
Swan Lake

牟尼沟花海 （摄影：隋山川）
A Sea of Flowers at Muni gully

左上图：水母雪莲 （摄影：蒲涛）
Top left：Snow Lotus Flowers
左下图：兜 兰 （摄影：邰永东）
Bottom left：Wild Cymbidium
中上图：野生郁金香 （摄影：邰永东）
Top in the middle：Wild Tulips
中下图：珊瑚菌 （摄影：蒲涛）
Bottom in the middle：Coral Mushrooms

右上图：高山杜鹃 （摄影：高屯子）
Top right：Azalea Flowers on a High Mountain
右下图：苞叶凤毛菊 （摄影：蒲涛）
Bottom right：A Kind of Indigenous Chrysanthemum

原始森林 （摄影：李宁）
Primitive Woods

左上图：小熊猫 （摄影：蒲涛）
Top left: The Lesser Panda
左中图：秃 鹫 （摄影：蒲涛）
Middle left: Cinereous Vultures
左下图：兰马鸡 （摄影：蒲涛）
Bottom left: Crossoptilon auritum
中上图：金丝猴 （摄影：蒲涛）
Top in the middle: Snub-Nosed Monkeys

中下图：藏马鸡 （摄影：蒲涛）
Bottom in the middle: Crosoptilon C.
右上图：猕 猴 （摄影：胡斌）
Top right: Macaques
右中图：云豹 （摄影：蒲涛）
Middle right: Snow Leopards
右下图：红腹锦鸡 （摄影：蒲涛）
Bottom right: Chrysolophus pictus

大熊猫 （摄影：蒲涛）
The Giant Panda

78

第 80－81 页图：辽阔的草原 （摄影：陈锦）
Pp80－81：A Grassland

第 82 页图：金碑夕照——中国工农红军长征纪念碑 （摄影：赵忠路）
Pp82：The Monument to the Long March of the Chinese Workers and Peasants' Red Army

左上图：春 （摄影：林义平）
Top left: Spring

左下图：夏 （摄影：隋山川）
Bottom left: Summer

右上图：秋 （摄影：高屯子）
Top right: Autumn

右下图：冬 （摄影：陈柯）
Bottom right: Winter

草原牧歌 （摄影：高屯子）
A Pastoral Song

温馨的生活 （摄影：林义平）
The Congeniality of Life

草原马帮的女儿 （摄影：杨恭洁）
Daughter of a grassland Caravan

抛撒风马旗,祈祝好运气 （摄影:高屯子）
Tossing the Flags for Blessings

松潘(古松州)古城　(摄影:龚威健)
Ancient City of Songpan

左上图：古城墙 （摄影：高屯子）
Top left：Ancient City Wall
左下图：映月桥 （摄影：杨继宗）
Bottom left：Moon-Silhouetting Bridge
右上图：村　寨 （摄影：胡斌）
Top right：A Village
右下图：清真寺 （摄影：高屯子）
Bottom right：A Islamic Mosque

第 94－95 页图：山林秋色 （摄影：何世尧）
Pp94－95：Autumn hue

《黄龙》编委会
主 任：冯友龙 陈钢 杜辉 胡斌
责任编辑：龚威健
撰 文：胡斌
译 文：凌原
地 图：傅马利
装帧设计：龚威健 陈正英
特邀摄影：高屯子 何世尧
摄 影：(按姓氏笔画为序)
于 宁 米文岐 杨继宗
杨恭洁 李天社 李 杰
李 宁 陈 锦 陈 轲
邰永东 周孟琪 林义平
泽仁珠 赵忠路 胡 斌
高 晔 龚威健 隋山川
蒲 涛 谭 明

图书在版编目（CIP）数据

黄龙/高屯子 何世尧等摄 . - 北京:中国
旅游出版社,1999.4
　ISBN 7-5032-1607-7

　Ⅰ.黄… Ⅱ.高… Ⅲ.风光摄影-摄影集-
中国-现代 Ⅳ.J426
　中国版本图书馆 CIP 数据核字（1999）第
08248 号

《黄　龙》

出版发行:中国旅游出版社
地　址:北京建国门内大街甲九号
邮政编码:100005
制　版:蛇口以琳制版公司
印　刷:新扬印刷有限公司
版　次:1999 年 4 月第 1 版
印　次:1999 年 11 月第 2 次
开　本:850x1168毫米　1/24
印　张:4
印　数:10001-15000册 004800

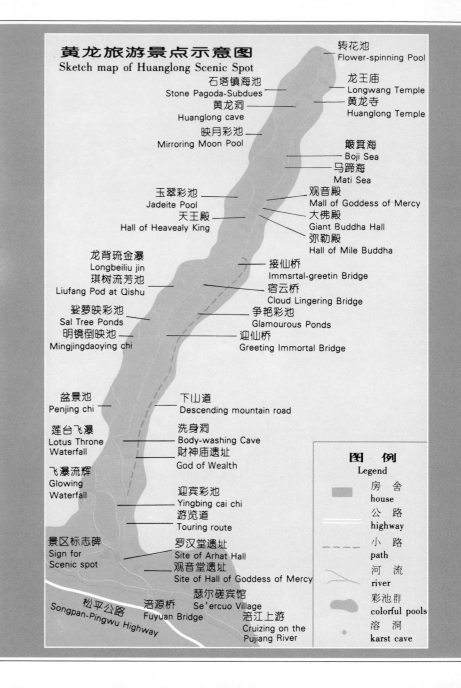

黄龙旅游景点示意图
Sketch map of Huanglong Scenic Spot

转花池
Flower-spinning Pool

石塔镇海池
Stone Pagoda-Subdues

龙王庙
Longwang Temple

黄龙洞
Huanglong cave

黄龙寺
Huanglong Temple

映月彩池
Mirroring Moon Pool

簸箕海
Boji Sea

马蹄海
Mati Sea

玉翠彩池
Jadeite Pool

观音殿
Mall of Goddess of Mercy

天王殿
Hall of Heavealy King

大佛殿
Giant Buddha Hall

弥勒殿
Hall of Mile Buddha

龙背琉金瀑
Longbeiliu jin

琪树流芳池
Liufang Pod at Qishu

接仙桥
Immsrtal-greetin Bridge

宿云桥
Cloud Lingering Bridge

娑萝映彩池
Sal Tree Ponds

争艳彩池
Glamourous Ponds

明镜倒映池
Mingjingdaoying chi

迎仙桥
Greeting Immortal Bridge

盆景池
Penjing chi

下山道
Descending mountain road

莲台飞瀑
Lotus Throne
Waterfall

洗身洞
Body-washing Cave

财神庙遗址
God of Wealth

飞瀑流辉
Glowing
Waterfall

迎宾彩池
Yingbing cai chi

游览道
Touring route

景区标志碑
Sign for
Scenic spot

罗汉堂遗址
Site of Arhat Hall

观音堂遗址
Site of Hall of Goddess of Mercy

松平公路
Songpan-Pingwu Highway

涪源桥
Fuyuan Bridge

瑟尔磋宾馆
Se'ercuo Village

涪江上游
Cruizing on the
Pujiang River

图　例
Legend

房　舍
house

公　路
highway

小　路
path

河　流
river

彩池群
colorful pools

溶　洞
karst cave